D0959070

Table of **Contents**

What Is the Skeletal System?

There are 206 bones in the human body! They make up the skeletal system.

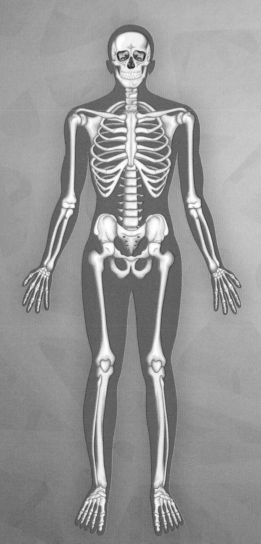

YOUR
BODY SYSTEMS

The Skeletal System

by Rebecca Pettiford

BLASTOFF!
3
READERS

BELLWETHER MEDIA • MINNEAPOLIS, MN

Note to Librarians, Teachers, and Parents:

Blastoff! Readers are carefully developed by literacy experts and combine standards-based content with developmentally appropriate text.

Level 1 provides the most support through repetition of high-frequency words, light text, predictable sentence patterns, and strong visual support.

Level 2 offers early readers a bit more challenge through varied simple sentences, increased text load, and less repetition of high-frequency words.

Level 3 advances early-fluent readers toward fluency through increased text and concept load, less reliance on visuals, longer sentences, and more literary language.

Level 4 builds reading stamina by providing more text per page, increased use of punctuation, greater variation in sentence patterns, and increasingly challenging vocabulary.

Level 5 encourages children to move from "learning to read" to "reading to learn" by providing even more text, varied writing styles, and less familiar topics.

Whichever book is right for your reader, Blastoff! Readers are the perfect books to build confidence and encourage a love of reading that will last a lifetime!

This edition first published in 2020 by Bellwether Media, Inc.

No part of this publication may be reproduced in whole or in part without written permission of the publisher. For information regarding permission, write to Bellwether Media, Inc., Attention: Permissions Department, 6012 Blue Circle Drive, Minnetonka, MN 55343.

Library of Congress Cataloging-in-Publication Data

Names: Pettiford, Rebecca, author.
Title: The Skeletal System / by Rebecca Pettiford.
Description: Minneapolis, MN : Bellwether Media, Inc., 2020. | Series:
  Blastoff! Readers. Your Body Systems | Includes bibliographical references
  and index. | Audience: Age 5-8. | Audience: K to grade 3.
Identifiers: LCCN 2018058078 (print) | LCCN 2018059266 (ebook) | ISBN
  9781618915641 (ebook) | ISBN 9781644870235 (hardcover : alk. paper) | ISBN
  9781618917560 (pbk. : alk. paper)
Subjects: LCSH: Skeleton–Juvenile literature.
Classification: LCC QM101 (ebook) | LCC QM101 .P39 2020 (print) | DDC
  612.7/51–dc23
LC record available at https://lccn.loc.gov/2018058078

Editor: Rebecca Sabelko   Designer: Brittany McIntosh

Printed in the United States of America, North Mankato, MN.

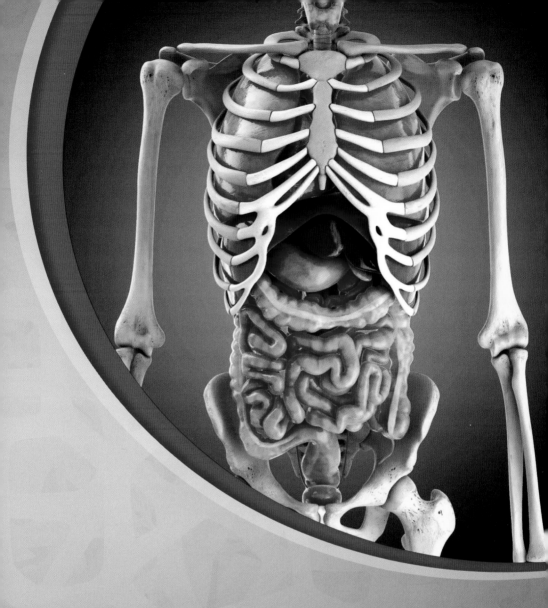

The skeletal system carries our weight and helps us move. It keeps our **organs** safe. It makes blood cells and stores **minerals**.

How Does the Skeletal System Work?

The skeletal system works with **tissues** to hold up the body and give it shape.

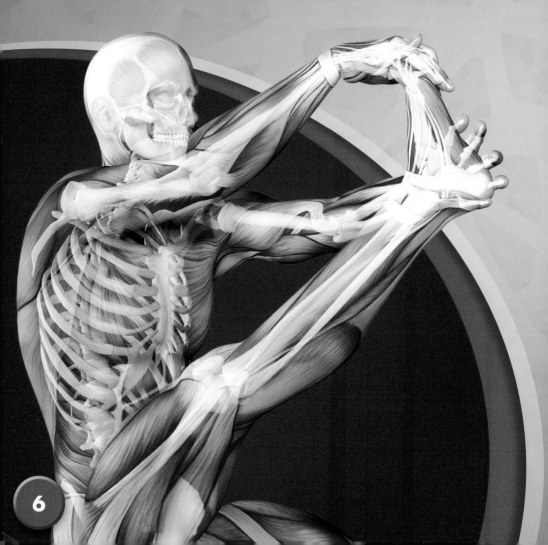

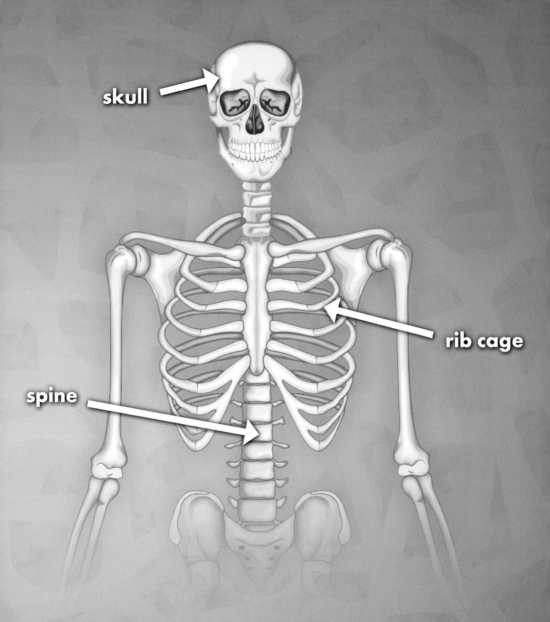

skull

rib cage

spine

Bones like the rib cage, skull, and **spine** give the body a base for other systems.

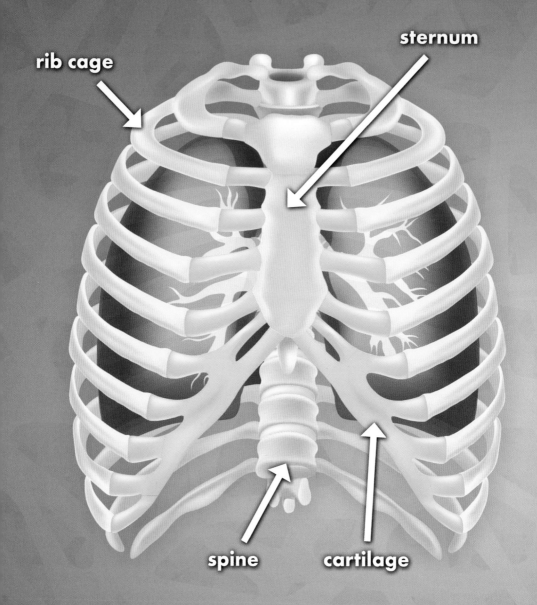

rib cage

sternum

spine

cartilage

Some bones keep organs safe.
For example, the rib cage hugs
the heart and lungs.

Tissues hold the ribs in place. **Ligaments** connect the ribs to the spine. **Cartilage** connects the ribs to the **sternum**.

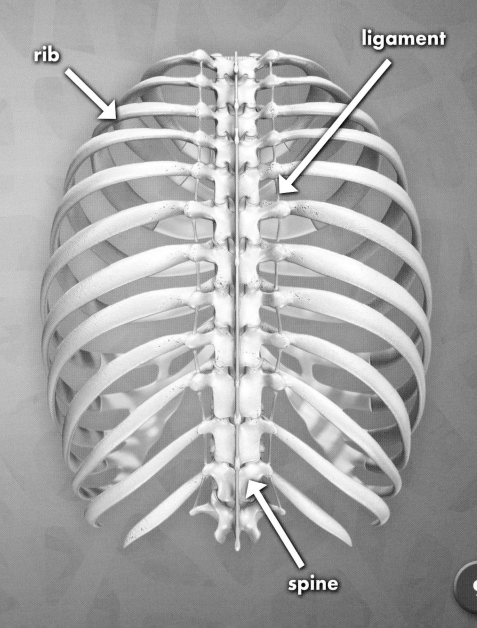

rib

ligament

spine

Bones in the arms and legs move the body. The skeletal system works with the **muscular system** to move **joints**.

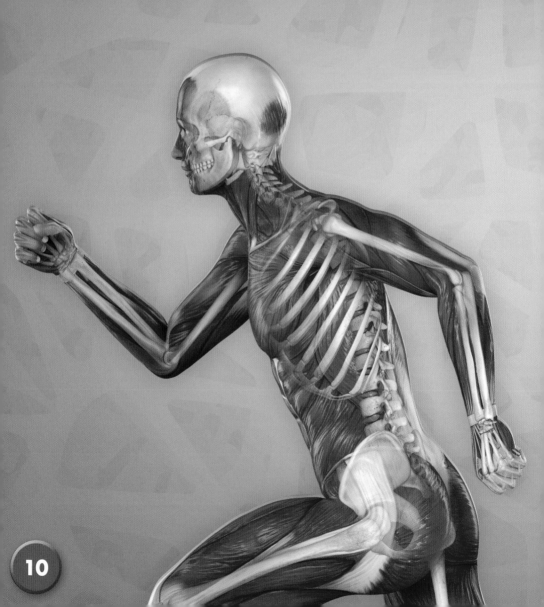

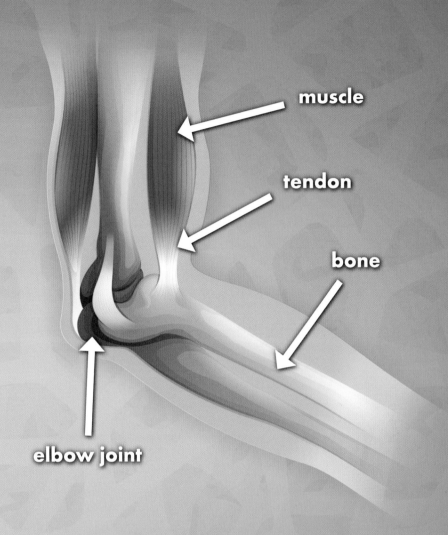

muscle

tendon

bone

elbow joint

Tissues called **tendons** connect muscles to bones. When a muscle tightens, tendons pull on the bone. This makes the joint bend.

The skeletal system stores minerals the body needs.

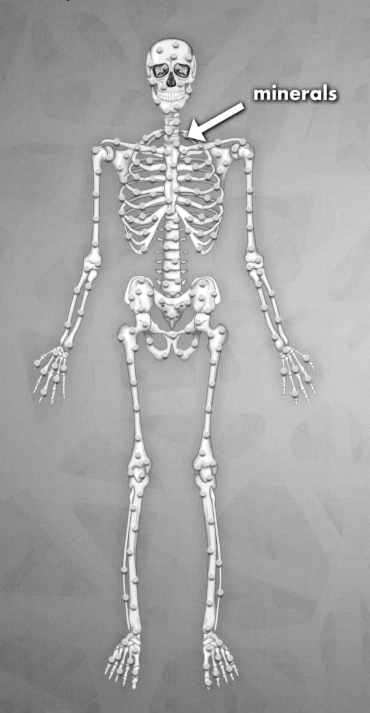

minerals

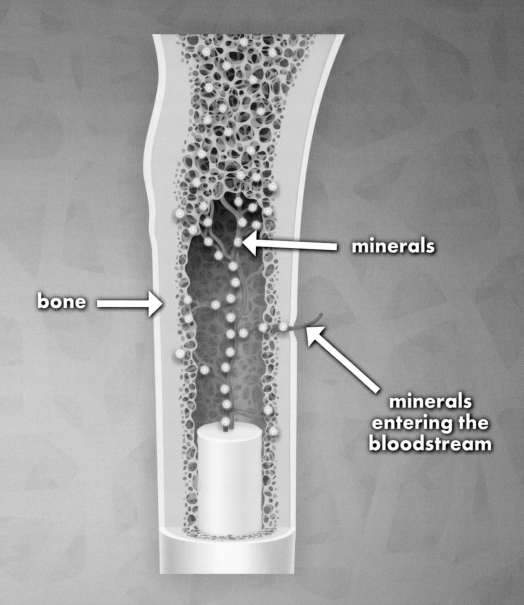

minerals

bone

minerals
entering the
bloodstream

When a part of the body needs
certain minerals, bones release
the minerals into the bloodstream.
The blood carries the minerals
to the body part.

calcium
in milk

Calcium is an important mineral for bones. It makes bones strong. It also helps muscles tighten.

If the body does not get enough calcium from food, it takes calcium from the bones. This can make the bones weak over time.

healthy bone

weak bone

The skeletal system also makes blood cells in bone **marrow**. Red blood cells carry **oxygen** throughout the body.

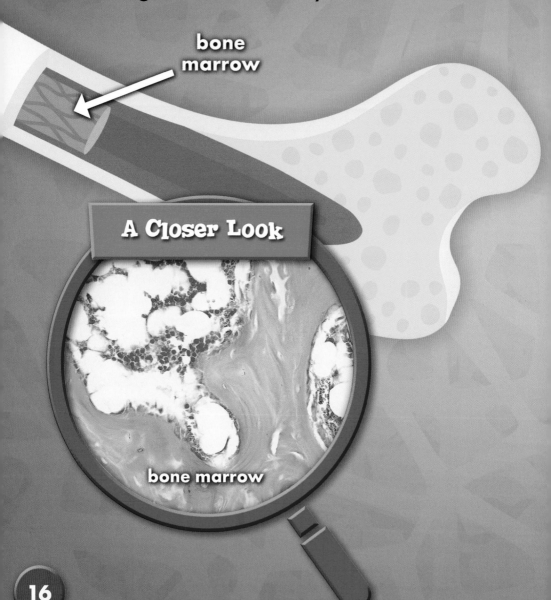

bone
marrow

A Closer Look

bone marrow

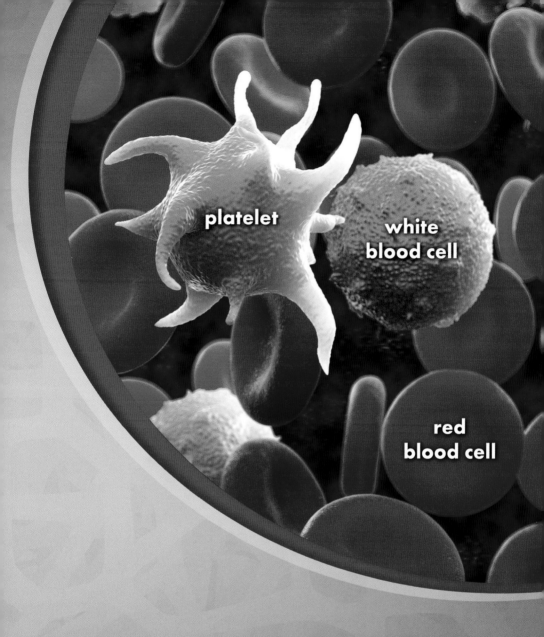

platelet

white blood cell

red blood cell

White blood cells help fight illnesses. **Platelets** help blood stick together to stop bleeding.

Why Is the Skeletal System Important?

The body would look like a pile of jelly without the skeletal system! It could not stand. It could not move. It would not have blood!

Your Skeletal System at Work!

Eating calcium-rich foods keeps bones hard and strong. See what happens when bones lose their strength.

You will need:
- two chicken leg bones with the meat cleaned off
- a glass jar
- vinegar
- plastic wrap

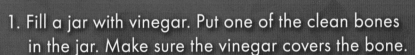

1. Fill a jar with vinegar. Put one of the clean bones in the jar. Make sure the vinegar covers the bone.

2. Put a lid or layer of plastic over the jar.

3. Wrap the second bone in plastic. Put it next to the jar.

4. After three days, remove the first bone from the jar. Rinse it off with water.

5. Try to bend the bone that was soaked in vinegar. Does it bend easily? How does it feel? Now, try to bend the bone that was not soaked in vinegar. Does it bend easily? How does it feel?

Vinegar is an acid. Soaking the bone in vinegar removes the calcium. This makes the bone weaker. It should be soft and easy to bend.

Exercise makes bones strong. It is important to keep your bones safe. Wear a helmet on your head. Wear pads over your knees and elbows.

Take care of your bones, and they will take care of you!

Glossary

calcium—a mineral that makes bones strong

cartilage—a strong and bendy material found between some bones

joints—points at which two bones meet

ligaments—tough pieces of tissue that hold bones together

marrow—the soft material inside bones

minerals—chemicals that are important for health

muscular system—the system that is made up of muscles and tissues that help move the body

organs—parts of the body that have a special purpose

oxygen—a substance in the air that is necessary for life

platelets—blood cells that help stop bleeding by becoming thick and sticky

spine—the column of connected bones down the middle of the back

sternum—the bone that covers the chest

tendons—cords of tissue that connect muscle to bone

tissues—minerals in the body that hold bones, muscles, and other parts of the body together

To Learn More

AT THE LIBRARY

Hansen, Grace. *Skeletal System*. Minneapolis, Minn.: Abdo Kids, 2019.

Kenney, Karen Latchana. *Skeletal System*. Minneapolis, Minn.: Jump!, 2017.

Pettiford, Rebecca. *The Muscular System*. Minneapolis, Minn.: Bellwether Media, 2020.

ON THE WEB

FACTSURFER

Factsurfer.com gives you a safe, fun way to find more information.

1. Go to www.factsurfer.com.

2. Enter "skeletal system" into the search box and click 🔍.

3. Select your book cover to see a list of related web sites.

Index

The images in this book are reproduced through the courtesy of: Sebastian Kaulitzki, front cover; Vecton, pp. 4, 7, 12; u3d, p. 5; DeryaDraws, p. 6; Studio BKK, p. 8; sciencepics, p. 9; cliparea custom media, p. 10; BlueRingMedia, p. 11; eranicle, p. 13; Littlekidmoment, p. 14; Disignua, p. 15; marina_ua, p. 16 (top); Wilson's Vision, p. 16 (bottom); royaltystockphoto.com, p. 17; Rob Marmion, p. 18; Coprid, p. 19 (plastic wrap); Garsya, p. 19 (bones); somdul, p. 19 (jar); AlenKadr, p. 19 (vinegar); Sergey Novikov, p. 20; VaLiza, p. 21.